1998

Storm

Judith Skillman

Storm

Blue Begonia Press • Yakima Washington

Acknowledgments:

I am grateful to the following journals where these poems first appeared, some in different versions:

The Iowa Review, "Tic Douloureux"
Poetry Northwest, "A Painter's Alphabet"
Prairie Schooner, "Asylum"
Northwest Review, "Anomalies," "Ornamental Plum," "The Indoor
        Garden," "This Could Be Zaydee's Birthday," "Black August,"
        "The Mole"
Exhibition, "The Robin"
Crab Creek Review, "Rookery"
Midwest Quarterly, "The Path Along the Ravine"
Fine Madness, "Winter Solstice," "Another Nutcracker"
Journal of the American Medical Association, "The Snags"
Mankato Poetry Journal, "The Starlings," "Hypochondria"
Silverfish Review, "Midwinter"
Kalliope: "Notes for Another Alice"
Laurel Review, "Want"

"Child," "Excursion," and "Daughterhood," were published in the Floating Bridge Press Anthology, *Pontoon*.

"Asylum" also appeared in *The Prairie Schooner Anthology of Jewish-American Writers*.

"Rookery" is for John Willson.

Thanks to the Centrum Foundation, for a residency at Fort Worden during which several of these poems were written.

My gratitude to Tom Skillman, Patty Cannon, Joannie Kervran, Tina Kelley, Marjorie Power, Michael Spence, Anne Pitkin, Joan Ross Blaedel, and Jack Gilbert.

Book design by Karen and Jim Bodeen
ISBN: 0-911287-26-4
Blue Begonia Press 225 S. 15th Ave., Yakima, WA 98902-3821

For my parents, Bernice Bloom Kastner and Sidney Oscar Kastner

CONTENTS

III. WANT

IV. THE ROBIN

I. THE THUNDERHEADS

"...a glance that grows blind from looking at itself
and sees blind,
a fire that is wild to go out,
a peace that wakes up storms,
a storm that brings peace...

    Ciril Zlobec, "Almost a Hymn"

ROOKERY

I too have an Uncle Jake
although he passed on
in the eighties. His hands shook
at the table and they were getting in the way
so my mother suggested he remove them.
In dreams the lack of a hand or a foot
proves to be no obstacle
but in real life it can be difficult
for a man like Uncle Jake
who was a nuclear physicist,
and needed to manipulate electrons,
especially those oddballs that possessed
an inordinate desire to travel from one shell
to another, deserting an otherwise happy molecule
to make hydrogen, argon, or helium.
In Styrofoam models
molecules seem stable, toothpicks hold
one ball to another,
but then there are always *sexceptions,*
which is a word I've just invented
and one Uncle Jake would've liked.
He would've laughed,
shaking like gravel
and Mother would cackle and look away
as the wire-haired terrier humped her leg
in their Kensington living room.
Never neutered, she'd whisper later.
Of all he said during gatherings of the clan
I can only remember
two things: *I wish I'd had more children.*
One's own dirt doesn't stink.

SUNDAY AFTERNOONS

What's left of the opera,
the colorful leaves strung on deciduous trees,
is only Mother
sighing as she says "They called him my little uncle."
She rights the shoes, thinking
absently of Sollie and Harold and the others.
In the old country house
crammed full of cousins,
she had a fever dream
when she was four. They came to comfort her.
But in the room the dream
still hovered. She remembers
how real it seemed.
A white tint in the sky, a row of droplets
herald the empty honor—
her father Izzy is born two years
after his nephews.
He goes to visit them
wearing a terry cloth suit, a nickel
sewn in his pocket.
Even as an infant he smells of fish.
How many relatives
can travel between the past and future
like he does? How many times
will the story be told
in all its versions?
Mother sits beneath a fig tree,
overweight and romantic in her plaids.
Her beat up suitcases
wait in the hall. Her face
floats against the olive oil tins—
a figment, a fragment.

THE MYTH OF A CHILDHOOD

Something small. A lemon
comes off in your hand.
You pierce thick skin and begin to suck.
Blue light stains the foliage of the tropics,
palm, yucca, eucalyptus
tighten against the sun,
and now your girlfriend's daughter
is walking into the garden,
turning on a sprinkler.
A trickle whets these trees
laden with Valencia's and grapefruits
heavy as the stones
Sisyphus hauled up a mountain
out of his love for discipline.
The sky milky and opaque,
heat beating in waves from the ground
as if a cusp of sun was buried here
and wanted now to break
out of the earth, extending fissures
in every direction.

MADRONA

Below her the straits,
and on the old military road
an occasional runner passes by
as she perches on steps of the fort.

Death is natural, yet the birds
avoid that madrona, the one
that begins as a solid trunk
and fans wide branches, twigs whittling
space into portions of air and water.

A great madrona with bleached limbs.
Unusual to see one of them gone up here.
As if there'd been a fire, or a drought.
When her lover leaves her she needs to visit
it to be certain it's still there.

Looks like a brain, he'd said.
She sits on the damp ground,
shouldering the strongest wood.

COMPLICATIONS

Sun cleanses needles of fir.
A few boughs broken by snow
lie distended in the yard, wet and yellow.

I meant to find the matter
still alive in heartwood.
It takes concentration
to come upon a complicated pregnancy
and find the shock of electricity lodged in the spine.

It is, after all, only afternoon.
A curve can be beautiful,
but not in the same way as a woman.

I sulk. In dusk light becoming winter,
in pink I find the accident.
A wedge of snow flutters
from the shoulder of the figure, like gauze.

Never mind incongruity.
This old house wants snow, lacks transitions
and lives on long silences.

I know how to take a scene
and make it play over and over,
a stack of records
black and deeply grained.

JUSTINE

Maybe his proclivity for work:
seven twelve-hour days back to back
broken only by the warden's knock,
and bread and water,
sewage backing up
in the makeshift hole,
perhaps she was a product
of this ugliness
more than any other.
It could be that captivity
fed his imagination, ripened
in a Paris prison
like a tree heavy with twinned fruit.
Plums and apples,
the pears that can't be saved, shaped
like women's bodies,
fallen once and for all
into sin for him.

And when the light grays,
whenever a man and a woman
lie like spoons
whispering casual obscenities
to one another,
his Justine returns
from her wood
to stand at the barred window
on tiptoe, gazing in
as if she alone forgave his mind
its excesses,
its cruel and pathetic fumbling.
Her wounds congealed, she stands
a long time
and leaves no imprint.

Maybe she is the only truly scentless creature,
woman who became an object,
rust-brown stains on her arms and legs.
So the warden's dog
sleeps on, though it runs
faster in its sleep.
She's found a way
to escape the tortuous turns
of his mind, she alone is fit to live
among the animals,
as vast and bad as anything
he could have invented.

NYMPHOMANIAC

Beautiful self, more than the others,
who took you,
let you go,
and wouldn't.

Lovely as a woman who moans.
Lying there,
an imprint. Who chose to die of want
or live in excess.

Posed like a pin-up girl
on tables, one leg
tied to a chair. Or
spread-eagled on a butcher block in the kitchen.

Say the words, as one girl
to another. Nothing's private,
there's nothing
that won't work tonight

to lift you
out of your head, that place
you live
among feathers.

JUNE

If a grown child departs, on her way
to an island so thick and green
it holds the future,
the daisies are impartial.
They can see all the way
up to heaven, and their white lashes
lengthen around plush brocade centers.
But they haven't any power
over their own lives.
He loves me, he loves me not,
petals stripped back
until the center quivers
like a spider in a torn web.
With the same heady scent,
by the hundreds, they develop
in slow motion
under the searchlight of a full moon.
Flowering was never a choice.
Eventually the cottonwood gives in to wind,
the girls grow breast buds
and the boys learn bad words.
Each year when the daisies
lean into one another
as if there were comfort
in being part of a crowd,
I hear their catty gossip
and I look forward to August,
cutting off their dry, shrunken heads
with my kitchen shears.

A PAINTER'S ALPHABET

Always
Bring
Cans to hold water,
Draperies,
Even light.
Full bouquets
Given already
Have potential as landscapes.
If you
Just
Knead their dry heads
Long enough
Mint will flower.
Nobody has to know
Or care if among your
Props you carry
Quilts,
Rainstripes,
Salt.
Trees might be
Understated, shaded
Versions of
Water within the long
X of perspective,
Yours, or
Zeus'.

EXCURSION

Found several dead trees.
You lifted bark
and showed me how a centipede
floats on wood,
told me how to tell
if per segment there will be two or four legs.
I got queasy
and observed that even
for the millipede
there are nowhere near a thousand legs.
You grew impatient, reminded me
that the number of legs
could be only two or four per segment.
The insect floated
as it walked. To pick it up
you used a leaf. Your father taught you
centipedes squirt acid.
We have to learn
to talk about these things,
the yellow line
so beautiful when the insect
flexes its incestuous muscle.

RANUNCULAS

I put them in a mason jar
and set them in the window.
They weren't buttercups.
Once you could have told me
anything, and I'd believe it.
Ranunculas have a jaunty look, petal
on petal, a few green buds
still full of the will to flower.
I bought them at Safeway
to make the cottage bright
for you and the child.
A little color splotched on the pane,
where rain was beginning
to splatter.   Yesterday Louise joked
about sliding down sheer white cliffs
to the water. She's the country mouse,
Jack says. Every so often she slips off
for a smoke. I can see the way
she smothers the corner of a building
with her desperation. Between smokes
she holds the cigarette lengthwise
in her palm, tipped away from me.
She doesn't want me to think any less
of her. I wanted to tell her
what I'd gone through
to keep you alive to the children.
Instead I bought ranunculas.
Their scent is like cheap perfume,
and no woman could be fooled
into thinking them roses.

THE THUNDERHEADS

All the leftover fatigue collects
in anvils and then, when it's time,
the anger comes. Lightning sears a madrona
and stitches its way into the ground.

I know where they come from,
the thunderheads, lined up, waiting their turn
like planes on a runway.
My father taught me what they were.

Each summer they crawl in a processional,
majestic. They carry the green fireball
to earth, they make a place for the box turtle
to stand between sewer and hedge.

I see them widen the gap between east and west,
hear my father cussing under his breath
as he stands with his collar turned up,
waiting and watching.

One storm will find its way
into a corner of the halfway state,
one swollen pocket of air take the gist
and bring it back to earth.

II. THE SPOILS

"Beauty is desired in order that it may
be befouled; not for its own sake,
but for the joy brought by the certainty
of profaning it."

Georges Bataille, *Death and Sensuality*

AS LOT'S WIFE

The caterpillar carries important messages
along sidewalks.
In suburbs layered across foothills,
down venues stroked by chimney smoke,
the caterpillar makes
a pregnant go-between.

This worm out walking in its coat of fur
under a brown sky,
the caterpillar, that numb pilgrim,
and the ant building a portcullis
in the dry needles are only insects.

The questions that make her want to see
the city she called home
at the moment of conflagration
are devils raised by the dust.

The caterpillar is a larvae
as dangerous in its shroud
as Lot's Wife, her muslin skirts
riffled by wind from the fire.

She has taken switch backs,
scrambled like a spider.
Sodom and Gomorra have nothing to offer.

The caterpillar walks the streets
in its orange and brown tuxedo.
Blood turns to salt
as the earth comes into autumn again
with its sticks, smoke, and stagnant news.

A creature of little meat,
the hundred legs swinging circles.
Even a centipede can feed the lost and hungry.

ANOMALIES

The sun comes up. I see it rise
through tangled branches and I know
this child is mine.

The ripest nest is an oval cyst
of sterile brown fluid,
a hollow vestige
like the sun. My heart
floats towards the center
of my chest, while thumping
deceptively on the left.

The richest gift is the one
that makes me different.
In the morning I put on
red cheeks, but come evening
I'll stand at the edge
and stare at a snarled vine.

I remember the day my husband
took the body of ivy
down from the chimney.
A woman with a flattened waist.
A reservoir for meals
of unhappiness. The outline
square as if still pressing against brick,
the venous organs beneath that gown
of outgrown webbing, just chalk.

And then he hauled her
across the yard, while she
kicked and screamed, deprived
of her amorphous
leafy child-flesh, a thick root
still spawning images.

THE SCALLIONS

Thin stems multiplied
in the garden, milk rose
in hollow tubes, carrying
remnants of a journey.

Perhaps it was September
and the year,
a foreign commodity,
balked and turned.

I was alone and sleepless.
Shutters opened
in the sterile room
and it was dawn, another morning

come to remind me of my sixteenth year
when the aged French woman
behind her stone walls
reprimanded me for being *une Américaine.*

I must have been just a girl
though my leather satchel
held the stink
of instruments and limbs.

The purple, starred flowers wanted me.
I was told to press my face
into the soft blur,
to hold my cheek against their color.

I had to bite down hard to be reminded
of a lover's flaws.
In raw bulbs
a sting and a slap, followed by

a dirge: the earth galloping closer,
swallowing my body.

EQUINOCTIAL MEDITATION

The equality of night and day
inspires temperance,
a man and a woman
spreading a blanket in an open field,
taking off their shoes and socks.

A bottle of wine sits in the grass,
jaunty neck angled like the mast of a ship
that's traveled from a year neither old nor new.
The flavor of sugar and cloves
suggests frivolity.

Another doorway looms.
So many distractions
for a skittish horse—screech owls,
guinea hens, and this scent,
which might be new paint,

the re-creation of a figure
floating on the ceiling of the Sistine Chapel,
a nude christened indecent
by the Pope.
Here come the breeches makers,

an army of amateurs
whose beards stir up dust devils.
Here's the sackcloth of winter
transferred to the genitals on the ceiling
by a censor.

RED-HEADED WOODPECKER

Tic tic. The woodpecker splays against
a madrona tree,
twitching madly,
wood and grubs flying.

Head jerks sidewise,
up and back. Three hops clockwise.
Stops, starts.
Checks for rot.

Fifty yards below
the sea pounds sand.
The sea sweeps the beach clean
and loads it with treasure.

White shale cliffs fossilized.
It's been ages
since the good doctor from France
made his forgotten diagnosis.

The woodpecker's a strange bird.
Hammers with its beak in cities
on metal street lamps
to attract the females.

I walk towards the crown
of the hill, the monuments
of war, struck
by the persistence of disease.

THE SPOILS

Leafing through.
The rake teeth, the handle
roughly in place.

She leans into the work.
Under leaves wetness sets in.
The fairy tale sun's yellow-gold no more.

Machiavelli's gift to the prince:
a few spare pages instead of cloth.

What if disease were there,
hidden like a stillbirth in the layers.

Suffocation or erotica,
the woman buried under a plethora
of receipts, earrings, gloves, sheets.

Today she worried. One kind of decay
begets another. She foists plots,
unveils conspiracies, discovers anger.

Hand shapes stay, pasted
under the broad tree
that will live through winter.

She wanted to call its branches *arms*
but that was wrong.

WASHING HER HAIR AT THE SINK

She lets the water run in and out
of her mouth, the taste of shampoo.
When they said *If you say that
one more time I'll wash your mouth out
with soap*, it wasn't the words
they wanted to get rid of.
It was something else.
Her hair tangles at the drain,
dark snakes like Medusa's. She wonders
did she lose her daring
all at once, or did the hard edge trickle
from her bit by bit.

STORM

He crawled into the pastoral
from the creek bed
and crossed a muddy stream
jumping like a fish,
exclaiming his own personal hallelujah's—
Shit.

There were stars
on earth too, networks
taller than he was,
and cattails patterned
a bronze field.

★

The tic, the blink.
Bad words under pressure.
They live sordid lives.

Fuck.

An endearment, almost.
Turned on its side,
a curse.

★

Then to understand
his love of storms.
The anvils
spreading out,
the synapses lightning
bridged, zig-zag.
Streaks discharging

their debits
in the great cathedral
of blacked-out cities
lit for an instant
by the grand culprit—electricity.

★

Inside our houses
we keep alive
the fear of water and heights.
Of certain colors and women.
The fear of spiders and numbers
and peanut butter.
The fear of fear—a disease
of idolatry.

★

To come by degrees
to the matter,
a fallen tree blocking the trail
like a corpse.
To learn forgiveness

as if it were a matter
of making such distinctions:
tufted titmouse, wren, swift,
and the barometer bird,
his mascot.

★

Grasses steam near the farm.
He leans into the eyepiece,
the comet stretched taut as a scar
in morning twilight.

Sirius, the dog star, blazing
as it does in time of famine.

*

I want to stitch grasses shut,
seam rushes
near the rookery.
His head's swathed
in the black hood
like a bird. He swears
at the machinery
of the family,
these constellations
that litter the sky.
In one a queen
lies on her side
seducing kings.

*

What sap,
what precious solder
holds the story together—
God the original father,
witness of planets, stars, and quasars.

Eater of soups
and exotic chocolates,
purveyor of salami and smoked meat.

In foreign delicatessens
an army of large women
waited on him.
The child who thought the world
was a clap of thunder,

an errant wire,
an antennae,
an insect buzzing,
let that child
remain in hiding.

★

Women from the Old Country took his order,
stood over their black bottom pots
coaxing broth to a hard boil.
He sat and ate his fill, drank

the teetotaler's cup.
Sidled back out into the street
and words spilled
from the hole in his face.

★

Who smothered the air,
drank from a pewter cup?

Who came later,
at the aftermath of the age,
clothed in ceremony?

If there was softness in him
it wasn't the familiar kind.

Above his head,
his craned neck,
eclipsing binaries.
One young star
intervening
on behalf
of another. One

would-be planet's
pocked-marked face
unmasking the sun's eruptions
around the edge
of a pink moon-disc.

★

Like a stroke
of summer lightning
he stands in the grass
near the Rose of Sharon.

Compass card, variable star,
the rosette on a shoe—
flowers exist
for the sake of reminder.

The hand mower
leans against a shed,
and lightning bugs turn on–off–on
serrated green bellies.

THE SNAGS

The ground pauses under their limbs
as they peruse its crushed cans, bits of paper,
and Styrofoam.

I can see their earthen beds, the dirt pillows
and hollows for knees and hips
where, legs elevated, they sleep
the short, uneasy sleep
of the dead, and wake
to strident crows, close in,
brushing soot off their faces.

They have assembled here,
my three dead uncles, garish in suede hats
and bleeding madras, gawky under the weight
of small rodents and birds who have made
their homes by complicated departures
and returns.

One of them with Parkinson's,
one with melanoma, and one whose heart
thickened, vessels stifled
by a stream of words.
Childhood's fast, red car

stops outside a hospital in Ottawa,
and my uncle the doctor gets out,
leaving us alone
while he goes in to birth a baby.
We play out an hour
apart from time, too happy
for what happens.

When I return my gaze

the snags have changed places,
pacing up and down
smooth passageways of forest carpet
like expectant fathers.

TIC DOULOUREUX

The trigger is sensation.

The violin's a dirty animal.

I want you to take away the suddenness.

Pain up the side of my head.

I'll have my teeth extracted one by one.

See if it makes any difference.

Rehearse for the real.

Be either present or absent.

I'll let my fingers drum ebony.

Thinking makes it worse.

I'll take the beat inside myself

and feel it up the center of my body.

A string through my head.

Imagine a hand pierced through the center by a wire.

I won't refer to Jesus or the crucifixion.

No blood in this exercise.

Let the hand move freely up and down this wire.

I'll wipe my nose when the bow

comes toward my face.

My head itches during the Vitali.

Lightning finds a way to enter the earth.

It's a pity music rises and falls.

Hide these bolts in a rock.

Insects carve sand trails as they enter the crab's eyes.

The thing of death is the animal knows when it's happening.

Leave a relic.

Any kind of pain.

A PATH ALONG THE RAVINE

Here Father clutches at sister's neck
and cusses softly—lichen on a tree
bears the imprint. His past grafted
to ours by an old woman stitching...

The handy leaves swallow light.
I'm a child in a German fairy tale—here Father
abandons us to a crone
who'll cage and keep us
for years, pinching the sticks
we thrust though bars. The moon
rises through conifers.
A simple lamp,
it blues the path.

In the crease we can hear
water rush past us. We know
we've missed the boat,
romantic spirits born too late.

Here Father gives us to the old woman
who lives in a tree trunk.
Her kitchen's close, we can smell
the tsimmis and carrots,
the bread rounded up like a leftover planet
approaching fullness.

I hold my sister's hand.
She's the plump child I'll sacrifice
in this version of the story,
her sticky ivory child-flesh
is what the tree holds in its slow tears:
a solstice present for our Mother.

THE FERRY FELLER

after "The Fairy Feller's Master Stroke," by Richard Dadd

Soldier, sailor, tinker, tailor.
A clodhopper with satyr's head.
Ploughboy, apothecary, thief—
even Titania knows
who stole a seed out from under Mother
to make a new carriage for Queen Mab.

The Fairy Feller, dressed in brown cords,
always on the verge, *tic tic,*
spinning clockwise, counterclockwise
ready to split a nut with his ax.

Watched by a horde of nymphs,
elves, and Spanish dancers,
By the harridan, the tatterdemalion,
the junketeer, and the dragonfly trumpeter.

Alors, écoutes, Madame de D.,
childhood disease goes on
years after childhood ends,
giving and taking its due with a vengeance.

★

Grasses hide the fairies and the elves.
Lubin is there, with his Chloe, his Phyliss.
The two dwarf conjurers
barely escaped with their lives.
Their short legs twitch.
Arms flailing, they pluck you from the air.

★

Are you still ill, Madame de D.?
De D., can you say,
"Six purple niggers riding in a carriage."
Can you see their wagoneer—
a small gray-coated gnat.

Ours is an autistic party,
driven by desire.
Can you crack that nut,
an empty hazel shell?

★

Madame de D, you look like Juliet
in your long black curls. *Viens ici,*
Come sit in the mirror,
skinny girl. *Chic* chick. I see you
in the beveled glass.
Be still Madame, whisper to me
from your cache of naughty words.
Say the old obscenities.

If you and I could be heard
apart from decent company—
the arch magician, the politician,
what shape our songs would take,
nasty echoes ticking from our lips, shapes
driven by the maestro's mouth.

III. WANT

"How to forget Persephone's pomegranate
grain in the coldness of winter?"

Marina Tsvetaeva, "Poem of the Mountain"

ANOTHER NUTCRACKER

after Li-Po

The moon-rabbit sits on earth
beating its balm,
there's no such thing as immortality
under a spindly tree,
only cinnamon and bark, the scent
of my mother's pies wafting
and then nothing, the door closing
on home—saddest of all
to leave that tableau
but then I never wore a tutu,
I was the jester
in Hoffman's mute opera
turning handsprings.
The crowd has no head
these short northern winter afternoons,
the hangmen come at four in their sharp black hats
to put out the sun.

THE PAPERWEIGHT

A house has found its way
into the snow.
I thaw from the center,
but the house is wood and stone.

Budging it requires
that I move into the paperweight
on the mantle.
In that numb place

I begin to grow afraid
of the others.
I send them away.
I'm swollen double, alone in dusk light.

The door of the house
changes to a stopper.
The birdbath's replaced by a wedding cake.
We live in a grim and terrible century,

I say, swaying
as I walk my huge body
out the mouth of the house.
I step off the porch

and begin to wind up
the sidewalk, a dirty string
attached to sky
as thick as water.

THE INDOOR GARDEN

The difference between this
and the winter beds
is that here currents of air still manage
to arrest the highest leaves, to lift them
without birds.

The same plant potted and repotted
becomes a tree. If a branch becomes sick
it can be severed and cauterized with tar.
Between a woman and a child
is a window that thickens with illness.

An inscrutable species
may perch in the neck of a bare tree
outdoors, but this garden makes do
with false moss and drinks
through a siphon.

I must be here again
because I am comfortable, the daughter
at my knee only reading, the hair I brushed out
this morning falling back into her eyes.
Gravel covers the roots of hyacinths

in clay pots. Nests in the trees
have pocketed their birds.
There are charts of anomalies
at the back of weather, behind
the arms of an orderly in white.

WINTER SOLSTICE

This time I'm a child of money,
my pockets full of soaps and pills.
Mother calls me home
to mend the rough places

in my voice, she calls me
to her sphere
with the voice of a preacher.
It's never too late,

you can still be Pollyanna,
she says, her face round
as sadness, broad as the winter
that stretches out before us both.

I have to remind myself
that ever since
her sickness Mother's been numb
as a button.

When I bury her
under fat flakes of snow
it will be winter.
Raccoons will come down from the trees

to gnaw those fishy stars
Mother planted in the ground
when she bonded to her nurse
in quarantine.

HYPOCHONDRIA

Out walking in fog,
the quarter moon
absorbed by branching trees
and, where the lung
stands empty, twigs.
How whole will you be?
Is the body to be taken on faith?
House waits to be occupied.
Each time you lift a fork
from the basket and place it in its coffin
on top of the others
colorless birds scatter,
lining birch tops
as if they heard.

WANT

They say a woman has no desire,
but still she rises at night
and waits at a closed door,
listening for clues. Even if it is
patriarchal, the train might sound forlorn,
passing through town one night
close to a man who sleeps through
and a woman who listens.
Its whistle inhuman as a comment I remember.
It had to do with her purse. Bulky.
No place to put it down. A luggage full
of tri-folded napkins, stained
with children, and he would have
nothing to do with it.
They say a woman has no desire,
but they don't see her there
at the top of the stairs, clutching
the thin robe around her shoulders.
No way to tell
when the bloody time will come
again, and break the spell
so she can feel, like an animal,
the shape of being held.

TEXTURAL VARIANT

When the man leaves,

leaves on the ground

focus sharply. These painted stars.

The brown day.

Tread on the stairs, tread

prints on carpet, a man

leaves. His departure

leavens the woman. She tastes

the flat taste inside her mouth

left by the man. She opens the pantry.

It's a careful day. The moth

with yellow clover wings comes

from its home on a shelf

into the kitchen,

where it will live for a year

printing soft embossments

all over her body, her face.

FAIRHAVEN

for Lisa

A little sadness waiting in the wings.
A bit like depression, that landscape.
It comes along the tracks,
a singing under the wheels,
in the brakes and belly of the train.
I remember you wanted to walk there,
where the curve became still more difficult.

THE STARLINGS

Deep in the tree,
so far in I can't see them,
a few starlings have risen
from their sleep to beat their wings
against the needles.

Why they fell asleep
in the afternoon
fastened to the crook of the tree
under the thin blade
of new moon is a mystery

just as it is a mystery
to come upon them
and startle them from their poses
beneath poisonous red garlands
that mimic summer berries.

They flutter and pulse
as if the peculiar
silence of winter
made them nervous,
as if they had contracted

the sickness of a grown child
returning home.

NOTES FOR ANOTHER ALICE

The ribbon of neck unravels as a child grows,
by notches, against a molding.

In order for her to stand up, the house must enlarge.
Its occupants are rabbits, mice, and winter flies.

Alice is one level removed from arts and letters so she can talk
to herself, taking both sides of the argument in turn.

The elbow she leans on prevents a door from opening inward.
A heavy ferry door, made to contain the force of water.

The sound of breaking glass in her house is the same
as in ours. Her hair catches in the limited light,

and her dress falls in folds of fairy tales, like the archetypal
mountain we walk towards, while investing in her ego.

The inmates of her house can go round and try the window,
but her arm fills it with another view.

Her mock breasts are stuffed under frills.
If she is left alone too long a piece of bread molds;

a rillet of penicillin blooms. Whatever she keeps to herself
it is well to remember there are other arrangements made for the sake

of convenience. The squares of her calendar change
overnight, to white lies. If she stretches and rubs like a cat

her fingers become mushrooms, their swollen tips prelude
to a difficult surrender. The spent coals, a cache of spare change or pebbles,

an attic of old laundry, none of this will turn to cakes
for her sake or ours. If she was never allowed

childhood, her pubescent body grown into a woman
before her time, then this is how she grows old,

by filling the house, sizing lace curtains to flowers
her shoulders lop off on either side. The dormer

of a house. Confined with her qualifying words
to the space allotted, she is keeping us.

THE MOLE

Was it five years ago
I thought you would emerge
as from a depression, blinking
black pupils dilated
from darkness or drugs.
Your fur lovely and dark
against your pink face.
Your feet small and correct,
and what big hands you had,
like the wolf in a fairy tale.
A sharp nose meant for burrowing.
I learned of your whereabouts
in the garden. The grass moved
to tell me where you were. Clay
the texture of chocolate cake
because the earth was catholic
then. Your mother saved
eggshells and coffee grounds,
pollinated tomato plants,
ate fish during Lent. Let's count
the longish nails of this effigy,
claws that bear the natural
numbers: one through five.
Touching it, turning it face down
with a tennis shoe.
Oddly human, wearing the wet coat
of afterbirth. What's your poison.
Trespasser in a handsome yard
crisscrossed by turkey wire.

MIDWINTER

A clear stretch. The cold
insular, the dish
turning under a stream of water
so its other face
can come clean.

The dipper slung low,
arranged exactly as before,
its bowl a sieve
through which admonitions
still trickle. The long handle

curving away from her, hiding animals
who live in the sky,
their fur vested with points
whose existence is
at best, theoretical.

IV. THE ROBIN

Nobody
bears witness for the
witness

Paul Celan

THE ROBIN

The robin's orange breast
is a sign. The way
it hops along the ground
under lucid trees
in the wake of Mother's letter...

In the round chest
I see a little heat
left over from the beginning of the universe.
Its luminous eye—
the black eye of a fish.

Dinosaurs and mammoths.
Antique flowers, sword ferns pressed
between leaves of shale,
species never recorded in the calligraphic annals
of the white man...

I think, and yes, if it is possible to be certain of anything
I would argue this fact:
the robin is coming across the grass
to tell me the macabre secrets
of its childhood.

A fairy tale about death, a story
of when it first scored the sky-blue egg
with the knife of its beak.
It cocks its head, as if to say,
Don't shoot the messenger.

BLACK AUGUST

There's an edge
to the child's fear
in August. I walk the trail
and hear her voice wander out of the house.

I hear her father smack her
to make her quiet, and then
I hear the small undoing,
and the increase.

I can hear all of this
and hike as if nothing was happening,
as if it were an accident,
the second blooming of a miniature rose

that depended on a sprinkler.
I pass by and touch the trunk of my tree
in my usual manner,
as if there were nothing odd

about the ritual in which I stop for an instant
and pose like Columbus,
looking out across the ravine.
I hear her voice wander

under my shirt
and think it hardly worth mentioning,
to be hot and sleepless,
to feel the beads of sweat on my forehead.

I plug my ears.
Then it's evening again
and I'm stuck in my slip, my hands
over my mouth as if I were

about to say something. I close my eyes.
It comes to me. I'm the one
who sees no evil, hears no evil,
and now you know the rest.

THE COMET

Night after night it pales,
peels back from you.
Deep in the sky, etched in the window,
though you hardly remember,
Ikeya Seki burns to the touch,
a scar you find close to sleep.

You close your eyes,
remember Father in Beltsville Field
standing under the black hood.
The hangman's come,
stepped out of a Florentine painting
to find you.

You dream a little,
get up, go to the window
and massage your breath into the pane.
Here's the platinum tail of a horse
swinging back and forth
to repel a summer's worth of flies.

Here's an instrument, a flower, a girth
that slides out from under.

You think of that plume,
Icarus' brief adolescence—
the feather, the danger
of riding or straying.

THESE STRAITS

Arms of kelp, old curmudgeon,
turning in early and late,
holding the shells captive,
and the ringing buoys.

Gulls perch on waves,
rain drums the cottage roof,
shears one hour from the next
and wets the new growth
shining from the rose. Water
slaps the waves and accumulates
in the well of a saucer
a man left at my doorstep today.

The sea lies dreaming of what it will not tell.
The sea delivers driftwood logs,
it smears the beach with jelly.
Like the rain,
it murmurs obscenities.

BENIGNANCY

The scent of magnolia
trapped in a pocket
close to the earth,
and this man visits
me in the evening,
his hair a white halo, his demeanor
mild. He speaks of his sex
distastefully. How few men
make good fathers,
though they are courted by the infant.
How certain a mother's love
for her child, and unconditional.
Human babies are born knowing
they need protection, in studies
they smile and coo
and sing to Daddy.
I spray my neck with perfume
after he leaves, and straighten
the lampshade. A dark splotch
where the bulb singed the round
skirt. I put my books
in neat piles and wash the last dish
by hand. Who can help me
if I stare a full minute
at the holly tree, those red berries
glittering between sharp leaves.
If the streetlight shines
into my bedroom
all night long, making me dream
of another pregnancy.

THE RUSHES

for Jim Bodeen

Certain waters braid,
others embroider.

Water crosses over, comes apart.
The path's a swath so brittle
they've paved it over
with new gravel.

I have to tend my thoughts.
This mass of voices—is it
the wooden beak of a bird
whose red head gives him away?

You say it is.
Certain waters braid,
embroider stories
to feed the little streams that amplify history.

Either way
the creek tumbles
its largesse, which consists of stones.

I overhear a story
about a monk—
grateful for stones
as he is for bread.
You take my picture at KFC.

How to fend off bitterness?
Even the rushes are embittered.
I can tell when I pass by
and hear their whispered,

gossipy messages.

You have boundaries.
I only have the rushes.
If anger is a gift, I'm rich.

I'll wander a little longer
among the voices.
Some I've come to recognize
as my own.

ASYLUM

A flutter of notes,
the *tic-tic* of beak on wood, and
a red-headed woodpecker tapping, knocking
at the door of a madrona,
looking for grubs.

Come in, I say.
Enter the tree, a feminine quantity.
Penetrate the mystery of daughterhood.

Always the soft fluff of forgiveness.
Always before or after a war.
In a deep wood flooded with memory,
the ticking, the twitching. Eyes everywhere,
etched in the bark of madronas,
on moth wing. In the decorative motion
of flower and bush, and the water
retreating from yards of beached wood,
I recognize the neurotic impulse.

But it's not neurosis anymore. In one
of Freud's dreams he lost a tooth,
and that tooth is the one we must discuss,
the way it fits in the palm
like a cigarette or a pill.

CHILD

They've gone and left you alone
with the empty beds and chairs,
the yellow Formica table a clean sweep,
standing on four legs
like an animal. Left you alone in this house
that lacks a foyer. Left you to yourself,
a child enveloped in the scent
of flowers sweating
close to the earth, a child who labors
to cross a small distance
like a potato bug, lacking the hard shell
of the bug and the instinct.
What was the child to learn
with its kindergarten fingers,
its kindergarten mind? That before
they left for the movies, grown-up
women clicked their high heels,
made up their lips and blotted them with tissue.
You fish one square of toilet paper
out of the trash. What can you say
to those red lips? What the disembodied
say when they talk to one another.

SEEING APHRODITE

It would have to be in a place
of war time preparations.

Deer grazing, unafraid,
and the brown black-spotted butterfly
that bears her name

flying at knee level.
Madronas on the bluff,

their trunks naked
and hard as stone.
This war over,

replaced by other wars.
No one whispers to make rain

or writes the name of God
on an apple, cuts the apple
into three pieces, and eats it.

Her shoulders mimic her breasts,
round and smooth.

This is how she was made.
A temptress from the beginning.
In her mind there are dirty words.

One of her eyes is blue glass,
one's a brown bud.

The brown one she borrowed
from a deer who wandered

unaware into her sphere.
She regrets having to kill.
A woman on a pedestal

must sometime step down,
crushing curls of madrona bark
under her thongs.

The arrow was taken from Cupid
after she seduced him.

To borrow an eye the second time is easier.
She uses the animal's fear
to excite her marble hands.

This kind of erotica
makes her almost human.

THIS COULD BE ZAYDEE'S BIRTHDAY

Any day now.
That hard Russian layered again like perpetuity
over a jagged French-Canadian and English.
Oy vey smere whispered over broken glass,
the symbol of hardship, like his stubborn silence,
wrapped in a towel and stomped on hard,
lifted towards the women
who dominated him with food,
with words.

We must have been the only children
who traveled north
like birds in the Springtime
to be served in his restaurant.
We sipped from bowls of clear soup.
Like ducks the soup nuts
floated and flocked.

He held confession
for his customers
while she stirred and ladled,
the dark curls escaping
from orphan braids,
pressed to her temples by steam.

Tonight I'll stand in the dark
and rub rough crescents
of moon between my fingers
until I remember why
they ate from one plate
even later when there was no reason to.

DAUGHTERHOOD

I could believe in dark trees,
the fire sighing as it goes out
under coals, wet and shrunken.
I could believe my mother
knew nothing all those years
she sat at the mahogany table
grading her papers,
that the wall phone waited
silent, without news
of medical advances
that could have spared Father
from a life of being a loner,
being teased. I could believe
in his thick lenses, glass
spun from sand and sugar.
Tonight I gaze through the window
after dinner, through the thickest
portion of the pane, where
distortion lives on,
happily ever after.
I see that wildflowers grow
in selfsame shapes
above the tree line. Clouds
are animals.   Each foreign country,
every riparian coastline
contains the same area,
peninsulas, deltas, and fjords
sharp as fractals
opening their complicated patterns.
Each new form
blooming like a curse.

ORNAMENTAL PLUM

What was said in anger that day,
and passed between the two lovers
who lie separated by time and distance
unravels slowly
as this tree does,
facing its portion of sky and water.

It owes so much to fruitlessness.
To the wind moving coldly
between branches,
the lamps and cars
winding along the freeway,
and the nothing new that can be said
about Spring or love.

Blossoms will slip from stems
and it will be summer again,
green leafing in between houses,
lengthening days. Whether the lovers
want to be stung by *yes* or *no*,
the tree stages its flowering
beside a road.

Because to be beautiful is the same,
but not quite, as forgiven.

NOTES:

"Justine" is a character in The Marquis de Sade's novel *Justine or The Misfortunes of Virtue*.

"Tic Douloureux" means painful twitch, and refers to trigeminal neuralgia.

"Fairy Feller" was written about the painting "The Fairy Feller's Master Stroke" by Richard Dadd. "Madame de D." refers to a seven year old girl who was one of Dr. Gilles de la Tourettes patients in 1885, and one of several patients to be diagnosed with Tourettes Syndrome before the diagnoses disappeared in the period from 1920-1970.

"Another Nutcracker" was inspired by Li-Po's "After an Ancient Poem," line 6: "moon-rabbit's immortality balm is empty..." The moon-rabbit refers to a Chinese legend in which there is a rabbit on the moon pounding a balm from the sap and bark of the cinnamon tree.

The line "We live in a grim and terrible century" in "The Paperweight" is borrowed from one of Thomas Merton's letters to Ernesto Cardenal, collected in *The Courage for Truth, Letters to Writers*, selected and edited by Christine M. Bochen.

"This Could Be Zaydee's Birthday" was written in memory of Israel and Leah Bloom.

The comet Ikeya Seki was visible to the naked eye in 1965 ("The Comet.")

"Benignancy" was written for Jack Gilbert.

ABOUT THE AUTHOR:

Judith Skillman's previous books are "Worship of the Visible Spectrum," Breitenbush, 1988, which received the 1987 King County Arts Commission Publication Prize jurored by Madeline DeFrees; and "Beethoven and the Birds," Blue Begonia Press, 1996.

In 1991 she was awarded a Washington State Arts Commission Writer's Fellowship. Commissioned in 1994 by the King County Public Art Program, Skillman wrote an original poem for the Jury Waiting Rooms Installation of the Kent Regional Justice Center, in collaboration with visual artist Joan Ross Blaedel and graphic artist Jesse Doquilo.

Skillman holds an M.A. in English Literature from the University of Maryland, and has done graduate work in Comparative Literature at the University of Washington. She teaches for City University in the Department of Business, Arts and Humanities.

ABOUT THE ARTIST:

Priscilla Maynard lives in Bellevue, Washington. An artist who has explored and taught in many media, Maynard has been working in Sumi on rice paper for over fifteen years. Sumi, she says, "is the most spontaneous, direct, soulful and soul fulfilling of all media for me."

Her Sumi painting on the cover of *Storm* is her second cover for Blue Begonia Press and Judith Skillman. Ms. Maynard"s "Wisteria", Sumi on rice paper, also served as the cover for Ms. Skillman's *Beethoven and the Birds*.

Priscilla Maynard has exhibited nationally and in the Northwest. Her work can be regularly seen at Foster/White Gallery, Kirkland; major collections include Robert Jeoffrey, Carl Bretten, The Northwest Watercolor Society, Nordstrom's and Rainier Bank.

Her degrees include M.F.A. in Painting and Art History from the University of Iowa, and B.F.A. in Painting from Wesleyan Conservatory.